WILDER GONE

Angela Hanks

BROADWAY PLAY PUBLISHING INC
New York
www.broadwayplaypub.com
info@broadwayplaypub.com

WILDER GONE
© Copyright 2023 Angela Hanks

All rights reserved. This work is fully protected under the copyright laws of the United States of America. No part of this publication may be photocopied, reproduced, stored in a retrieval system, or transmitted, in any form or by any means, electronic, mechanical, recording, or otherwise, without the prior permission of the publisher. Additional copies of this play are available from the publisher.

Written permission is required for live performance of any sort. This includes readings, cuttings, scenes, and excerpts. For amateur and stock performances, please contact Broadway Play Publishing Inc. For all other rights please contact the author c/o BPPI.

Cover and text design by Amy Marie Huber
"Aunt Tee" photograph provided by Carl Hanks from the collection of Carl Hanks

First edition: March 2023
I S B N: 978-0-88145-967-8

Book design: Marie Donovan
Page make-up: Adobe InDesign
Typeface: Palatino

WILDER GONE was commissioned by Clubbed Thumb, made possible by The New York State Council on the Arts, with the support of Governor Andrew Cuomo & The New York State Legislature. The play was developed as part of Summerworks in May of 2018 by Clubbed Thumb.

WILDER GONE received its world premiere at Clubbed Thumb (Maria Striar, Producing Artistic Director; Michael Bulger, Associate Artistic Director) in New York as part of Clubbed Thumb's 2018 Summerworks on 4 June 2018. The cast and creative contributors were:

THALIA NEWSTROM .... Toni Ann DeNoble
MABEL JENNINGS .... Crystal Dickinson
REVEREND JOHN JACK .... Washington Kirk
DOTTE LANGFIELD ....Nicole Lewis
OLIVER OAK .... Christopher Livingston
STREETER HENLEY .... Hubert Point-Du Jour
PEANUT BRITTLE .... Markita Prescott

Director .... Margot Bordelon
Scenic design .... Reid Thompson
Costume design ....Beth Goldenberg
Lighting design .... Marie Yokoyama
Sound design .... Kate Marvin
Production Stage Manager ....Rick V Moreno

WILDER GONE is dedicated to the memories of my mother, Lana Jean Sherman Hanks; my grandmothers, Tommie Mae Sherman and Anthony Renée Hanks; and my paternal great-grandmother, Arista L Hardeway.

CHARACTERS & SETTING

THALIA NEWSTROM, *a biracial woman of African-American and German descent. She is rather headstrong. 29.*

STREETER HENLEY, *he has been sweet on* THALIA *for most of his life. He is on the cusp of 30.*

MABEL JENNINGS, *she aspires to be a preacher. 39.*

REVEREND JOHN JACK, *A charming man. 32.*

PEANUT BRITTLE, *she serves as* MABLE JENNINGS' *right hand woman. 12.*

OLIVER OAK, *a friend of* PEANUT BRITTLE. *14.*

DOTTE LANGFIELD, *a palm reader residing in Ellum; brothel madam is her side hustle, sometimes. 40.*

All roles are to be played by an entire-Black cast.

1921
Dallas, Texas
a piece of land uncultivated
Wilder Street
DOTTE's *home*
Various Dallas

A NOTE ON TEXT

When two characters names appear side-by-side, the dialogue is spoken simultaneously:

THALIA:	STREETER
(dialogue)	(dialogue)

When multiple characters' names appear on page—on a horizontal plane:

THALIA:
(dialogue)

    MABEL:
    (dialogue)

        STREETER:
        (dialogue)

The dialogue is spoken in quick succession to create a measured polyphony of voices. This may look a bit like sheet music, in form.

(1921)

(THALIA NEWSTROM *is yelling out in exhilaration at the
big, blue sky.
She wears a nice hat and a mink stole, as she stands on
Wilder.
She picks up a rock.
She throws the rock in the direction of a tuxedo cat.)*

THALIA:
And no cats on this property.
(She looks out across the yard, and begins to wave wildly.)
Hello!
Hello!
(She continues waving, in absolute earnest.)
Hello!
Hello!
*(She scrunches up her face, confused.
She gives the middle finger and smiles broadly.)*
What a lovely woman. What a lovely welcome.
This is home, surely.
(She inhales deeply.)

(The tuxedo cat crosses her path again.)

THALIA:
But, absolutely no cats!

(THALIA *picks up another rock, and aims it for the tuxedo
cat, but the cat runs away in time.)*

THALIA:
But, two stories. At some point.
(She starts to do something little weird, she knows she

is outside, someone could quite possibly be watching her
now, but she also feels as if she is in the world alone, at the
moment. Even so.
She does a little dance, maybe.
A discrete sway of the hips.
She feels the breeze on her cheek.)

(STREETER HENLEY *comes on with a wheelbarrow full of*
dirt.
He stops to watch her.)

(THALIA *picks a dandelion.*
She blows on it releasing its seeds into the atmosphere.
She watches the floaters in the air.)

(STREETER *likes this very much.*
He continues to watch THALIA, *then:)*

STREETER:
Thalia.

(THALIA *lets go of the dandelion.)*

THALIA:
Streeter.

(THALIA *and* STREETER *stare each other down for bit,*
squaring off,
and then:
both smile.)

STREETER:
Is this it?

THALIA:
Yessir:
lot Wilder.

(STREETER *pours the dirt onto the grass.)*

STREETER:
It is overgrown.

THALIA:
Then we will cut down all that.

STREETER:
You are going to cut this wild, wild land?

THALIA:
I will.

STREETER:
And folks will be able to tell you are straight up
country.
A city lady does no such thing.

THALIA:
This one will do such a thing.
I will wear a big straw hat, keep myself out of the sun,
somehow.
You should get yourself one, too, if you wanna stay a
shade below.
Look:
I have already met us some new neighbors, that
woman and child there yonder.
(She gives the finger again.)

STREETER:
What is all that?

THALIA:
Saying, "hello", the city way.

(STREETER does the same.)

*(THALIA and STREETER stand there, solidly giving the
middle finger.)*

THALIA:
Hello!
Hello!

                              STREETER:
                              Hello!
                              Hello!

THALIA:
We have to do something about these damn cats.
Do they not have homes?

STREETER:
This is their home, Miss Newstrom:
Leave 'em be.

Where we gone start to cut?

THALIA:
We can start right here.

(Pause)

> THALIA:
> Cats:
> are not like us.

STREETER:
I suspect not.

THALIA:
They are not anything like us. They leer. They creep.
They jump with no caution given.

STREETER:
Every single thing a cat does is in a graceful, calculated
way.
Bears resemblance to your own inclination.

THALIA:
Are you comparing my inclination to that of a cat?

STREETER:
I am.

(THALIA kinda grins at this.)

THALIA:
Come on, kid.
Let us go get our suitcases from the car.

(THALIA and STREETER head off.)

*(Moments after, several plots over from where THALIA has
been feeling her claim,
MABEL JENNINGS stands, out in her own yard,
at a makeshift pulpit preaching*

to a congregation of one.
Her name is PEANUT BRITTLE.*)*

MABEL:
And you will know us by the trail of good souls that
we have left behind.
And you will know us by the stories, handed down
from generations to generations, that tell of our
inherent graciousness.
And you will know us by the care we did take to till
the land, to guide the souls to righteousness, and to
dispel the devils makings from our very own lives.
And you will divine from us the goodness that we
bestowed upon the saved.
And you will understand that you, too, can be saved!
Exonerated! Liberated!
By the mercy of God and our Lord Savior Jesus Christ,
you can be saved!
(Pause)
Can I get a amen, Sister Peanut?

PEANUT:
Amen, Sister Peanut.

MABEL:
Thank ya, Jesus:
You are the one the only one who can ease my troubles,
cease my worries, and redeem my sins.
Hallelujah.
Thank ya, Jesus.
Now, I heard of a woman who did bear a child out of
wedlock.
Yes y'all, she bore a baby.
Out of wedlock.
(Pause)
I inquire to her, "Sister, where did you go wrong?"
She looked at me with them big brown deer eyes,
brimming with tears, full of shame and regret,
and wept.

I took her face into my hands, wiped away some of that misery, and pressed on.

And this is what she tole me, and this is what I am tellin' y'all, right now:

I was born a lover;
I was born a fighter.
But my body gave way,
and I felt defeat.

(PEANUT *takes out a tambourine and taps it lightly.*)

MABEL:
But my sin gave way.
And without delay,
I found myself with child.

You see what I mean, y'all? Let me interpret for the peoples:
she took action upon temptation.
Imma say it only once:
you have got to control yourself and your urges.
They ain't ready for it yet, Sister Peanut. What you think?

PEANUT:
They ain't ready.

MABEL:
Are you ready for this good speech, Sister Peanut?

PEANUT:
I been ready since yesterday.

MABEL:
Alright now.

PEANUT:
Sister Mabel?

MABEL:
Sister Peanut?

PEANUT:
You did not finish the song.

MABEL:
I have switched to speechifying now.

PEANUT:
But, I wanna know what happened next.

MABEL:
She got pregnant out of wedlock, sugar.

PEANUT:
But, I wanna know how. The details; the particulars.

MABEL:
It just happened, Peanut Brittle.

PEANUT:
I do not think so, Mabel Jennings.

Now, there are things about procreation that I wanna
know about. And, something tells me it is in them
lyrics. And, I wanna know how and why.

MABEL:
That is grown folk's business.

PEANUT:
I became a woman three months ago today. I am not a
little girl no more.

We have gone over all this.

MABEL:
Ain't school tomorrow?
(She chucks back the rock THALIA *threw.)*

PEANUT:
Yes'm, it is. And I will be going. There is a geography
test tomorrow; and geography is my best subject, and
my favorite subject, and I am sure to make good marks
on it.
(Pause)
Now, back to this song about procreation. Did that

woman derive any pleasure from contact? Cause I
heard that pleasure is something only the mens can
experience, but Dotte Langfield who live out Ellum
yonder told me different.

MABEL:
I think you be best off if you stay away from Dotte
Langfield.
She runs hussies.

(No beat taken)

PEANUT:
She got good ham.

MABEL:
And who knows where she got it from.

PEANUT:
She got it from her peoples down in Marlin. She go
there once every winter and they give it to her, but
they do not ask no questions about her life in the city,
and so she offers no further information. She just put
on a Sunday hat to make her look right nice. No color
on her lips, either. Just plain.

(A rock lands in front of PEANUT.)

MABEL:
Lord, help the child whose curious nature will surely
land her in asylum.
Why in Jerusalem does she keep throwing rocks over
here, like I am David and she is Shimei?

PEANUT:
Are you gone flash your finger at her again, Sister
Mabel?

MABEL:
When did I do that?

PEANUT:
Oh, I saw that, for sure.

And, I heard what you was saying, Sister Mabel.
(Pause)
But do you not think that odd though?

MABEL:
What?

PEANUT:
If you is talking to the Lord Savior, I should not be able
to hear your thoughts when you is talking to him in
privacy. Am I wrong about that?

MABEL:
Yes.
(She throws the rock back to where it came from.)

(A crash)

PEANUT:
You hit the new neighbor's windshield.

MABEL:
Shit.
Run behind this pulpit before they spot that it is
cracked.

(MABEL and PEANUT run behind the pulpit.)

*(Meanwhile, THALIA has been letting the dirt run through
her fingers.)*

THALIA:
Might not be able to do nothing with all this mess. Feel
this.

STREETER:
Just gotta tame it a bit.

THALIA:
It needs a transfusion for sure.
The best damn soil is setting outside my old home in
Waller County.

STREETER:
You might maybe be right about that.

THALIA:
Definitely, the best damn soil.
*(Her eyes suddenly widen and she inhales sharply, making
a curious sound. She looks at* STREETER *with a quiet smile
until it becomes somewhat disturbing.)*

STREETER:
Oh, what now?

THALIA:
We gotta go back to the country for the rest of the soil.
I want all of it.

STREETER:
Nope.

THALIA:
And why not?

STREETER:
We brought the one wheelbarrow full only. That was
the agreement. That is what we could manage.
Besides, how in Moses do you think we gone get the
rest of that soil from Waller to Dallas?

THALIA:
We will need a truck.

STREETER:
We have no truck.

THALIA:
I can get us a truck.

STREETER:
How?

THALIA:
We will trade out that Tin Lizzy for it.

STREETER:
Will you just marry me instead? It is the easiest thing
to do.

THALIA:
I hate easy.

(Pause)
Look:
Just ask me again sometime next month, maybe.

STREETER:
You say that three year ago. Then again, a week ago.

THALIA:
Well, we are older now, and I feel little more settled in
my life, but only a little.
So, catch me again next month when I feel that real
adult shit some more.
(Pause)
Where is your sense of adventure?

STREETER:
I do not have one of those.

THALIA:
You used to.

STREETER:
I am an old man now.

THALIA:
Oh, please, boy.

STREETER:
Thalia.

THALIA:
Streeter?

STREETER:
Do not call me that.

THALIA:
You are behaving as such.

STREETER:
Boys do not settle immediately with women they have
affection for.

THALIA:
That word.

STREETER:
Affection?

THALIA: *(Immediately)*
My good stars in Heaven, Street:
why you in a rush?

STREETER:
Who knows if I will make thirty-five.

THALIA:
You are such a worrywart, man.

STREETER:
That is much better.
Thank you for that.

(Pause)

THALIA:
I can always go back myself. I do drive.

STREETER:
I cannot let you do that.

THALIA:
I know the way, Street.

STREETER:
I know you know the way, Thalia.

THALIA:
So, you want to come along then?

STREETER:
Follow you up, follow you down…

THALIA:
Then you are okay with me going by myself? Is that
what I am hearing?

STREETER:
Come over here, please, ma'am.

(THALIA *does not.* STREETER *goes to her.*
He stands directly in front of her, matching their toes up.)

STREETER:
Look at that:
we do literally go toe to toe.

THALIA:
Well, if that is not just as sweet as a peppermint stick.

STREETER:
I thought so.

(Pause)

THALIA:
That soil is there for us to take; not a one body is
guarding it.
I just want the soil; the house is long gone from me, but
the soil is mine.
I can have that, at least. Can I not?

(STREETER *relents.*)

(THALIA *howls at the sky.*)

STREETER:
Feel better?

THALIA:
Good Moses, yes.
(She picks up a rock and chucks it in the direction of the cat.)
Close. Very close.

STREETER:
That cat ain't thinking about you, Thalia.

THALIA:
(She whoops at the sky, like before.)
Are you the cat expert? Did you go to school on it?

STREETER:
I do not think cats crave humans. At least, not live
ones.

THALIA:
What do you mean by that exactly?

STREETER:
A cat would only find interest in humans who have
been dead for some time.

THALIA:
Then I suppose I will never die.

STREETER:
How are you gone pull that off?

THALIA:
I will leave this plot of land to my grandchildren. And
then, they will leave it to their grandchildren. And then
on, and then on, and then on.

I will never die.
(She feels a slight breeze.)

*(*OLIVER OAK *stands there with a newspaper.)*

OLIVER:
Newspaper, ma'am?

THALIA:
What, did you just appear from the thin air?

OLIVER:
This is my route.

STREETER:
This is a route?

OLIVER:
Yessir. Neighborhood may be mostly vacant, but I still
gotta serve the papers.
You wont one?

THALIA:
Sure.

STREETER:
How many folks you deliver papers to in this area,
son?

OLIVER:
Usually about twelve.

THALIA:
Twelve only!

OLIVER:
Yes'm. Not much, but the city on the rise.
Three pennies.

THALIA:
In the country, it is one cent.

OLIVER:
I do not know nothing 'bout the country, ain't never
left this city my whole entire.
(*He holds out his hand.*)
Thanks, ma'am.

STREETER:
You welcome, son.

OLIVER:
Are you my daddy?

STREETER:
I, no.

OLIVER:
Oh, I thought maybe you were, you kept calling me
son, and I felt affinity.
He left such a long time ago.

THALIA:
We are sorry to hear that.

OLIVER:
One day I find him.
(*He stands there, nodding.*)

THALIA:
If one is inclined, where does one get a nice, cool drink
in this city?

OLIVER:
If you wont you can go to the five- and- dime on Pine
Street.
(*Pause*)
But if you wont something stronger, head a little ways
west of here.

STREETER:
We will need something stronger.

OLIVER:
You gone drank with him?

THALIA:
Oh, I plan to, yes.

OLIVER:
Is you allowed to do that? Is that allowed in the
country? Maybe that is allowed in the country?
I just have never been. Is that allowed in the country?
Is it?
Maybe it is? I just never seen it in my entire fourteen.
But, maybe it is okay? Is it okay to drink, with him, in
this city? Without recourse? Or a side eye, at least?
It is just that:
I thought you was a white lady, for sure.

(THALIA *is silent.*)

OLIVER:
It is fine, ma'am. Sometimes, I have troubles saying
things, too.
(*Tiny quick*)
Welcome to Queen City.

THALIA:
That is truly kind of you.

OLIVER:
If you say so.
(He leaves.)

STREETER:
No wonder his daddy done left him.

*(*THALIA *and* STREETER *snicker a bit.)*

THALIA:
Oh, but Queen City! If the neighborhood do fit.

STREETER:
Oh, please, girl.

THALIA:
I feel like one, right now, in this very moment.
I just walked right up on in there.

STREETER:
Teller did not even take a double, you looked real
society. And all.

THALIA:
Came out a victor.
By all accounts:
I own this patch of land.

STREETER:
Maybe, eventually, ours one day…

(Quick and over)

> *(*OLIVER *delivering the
> news, behind the* MABEL's
> *house.)*
>
> OLIVER:
> They from the country.
> She own that claim, y'all.
> She gone leave that plot of
> land to her grandchildren
> when she die.
> She hates cats.

MABEL: PEANUT:
Oh, hell, no.   Ooooo!
How did that happen?
Kessler told me that land
good as mine.
I mean, shit.

PEANUT:
God gone strike you down,
Sister Mabel.

MABEL:
Cursing is only allowed
when someone sets sights
on your territory.

OLIVER:
Real now?

MABEL:
Deutoronomy 19.8.

OLIVER:
Oh, snap.

(PEANUT *shakes her
tambourine.*)

MABEL:
Here, have some taffy for
your snooping.

(MABEL *throws* OLIVER
*some taffy.
He chews on it.*)

(Back)

THALIA:
March is on the rise:
your day approaches steadily.

STREETER:
…Yes'm.

THALIA:
We gone make it extra special this year, Streets.
This birthday is a magnificent achievement.

STREETER:
Thalia, I am not sure my turning thirty is such an
achievement.

THALIA:
It is the living part that matters most, dear Street.
I will make your favorite:
gooseberry cobbler.

STREETER:
That is my favorite.
Thank you.
(He kisses her softly on the cheek.)
Feel that sunbake.

*(THALIA lets up her parasol. She touches the spot on her
cheek where STREETER has kissed her. She has a quiet panic
attack.*
*They have been staring at the horizon for quite some time,
and then, noticing her shaking:)*

STREETER:
What is all that?

THALIA:
I feel like I have glimpsed my future bleak.

STREETER:
Oh, it cannot be all that.
Wasn't I in it?

THALIA:
Let us set out to Waller before the afternoon.
(She is off.)

STREETER:
Wait, what?
(He watches her go.
He follows.)

(Peanut comes from hiding behind the pulpit,
with Mabel behind her.)

Mabel:
Where they at?

Peanut:
They headed out real quick, Sister Mabel.

(Mabel gathers up her church things, makeshift pulpit and
all.)

(Peanut's stomach growls.)

Peanut:
I am hungry.

Mabel:
Do they not feed you at the boarding house?

Peanut:
If I do not wake up at the right time, and set the table
and get to the table, someone always takes more than
their share.

Mabel:
Maybe someone thinks since you so skinny you don't
eat much no ways, no how.

Peanut:
They do not know my appetite.
(Pause)
I could not find a pail to wash those cloths out this
morning.

Mabel:
Baby girl, just take a pail from the stables and have it in
your room for you only.

Peanut:
But that is stealing.

Mabel:
It is surviving.
(She puts her hands in the air,

and closes her eyes.)
I survive by acknowledging that I am not perfect in His eyes.
And He lets me know that he accepts my bid for self-preservation through His divine touch.
I dreamt that I am the conduit that allows for God to reach folks; no longer a laundress, in this dream,
I am more.
I have a purpose on this earth beyond the corporeal;
I have a purpose beyond all that soap.

REVEREND JOHN JACK:
It is not a bad purpose to have.

PEANUT:
And who in Moses are you?

REVEREND JOHN JACK:
John Jack.

PEANUT:
Why you wearing that big-rimmed hat? You been preachin' a sermon, too?
Only preachers wear them types of hats.
(He tilts his hat.)
Sister a Mabel a preacher, too.

(MABEL has fallen silent.)

REVEREND JOHN JACK:
I ain't never met a woman preacher before.

PEANUT:
She gone be the first in Dallas, and I am gone bear witness to it.
The suffrage passed a year ago, and I ne'er thought I would live to see that day:
it is just a matter of time now before womens get to do whatever the hell we wont.
(Pause)
What you got in that satchel? Your life's worth?

REVEREND JOHN JACK:
Just about.
Just bought a newspaper.

PEANUT:
Then you have met Oliver Oak.

REVEREND JOHN JACK:
Is that who that was?

PEANUT:
Yessir. He only live with his mama.

REVEREND JOHN JACK:
And what is your name?

PEANUT:
Peanut Brittle.

REVEREND JOHN JACK:
What is your real name?

PEANUT:
They been callin' me Peanut Brittle my whole twelve,
and that is all I go by, and that is all I will respond to.

REVEREND JOHN JACK:
I accept that.
(*Pause*)
Any leads on where I might wash up, Peanut Brittle?

PEANUT:
I would suggest my own boarding house, but that
man from Alabama ain't left yet. He sound like he got
marbles in his mouth when he speak, so I thought he
was drunk all the time, but he ain't drunk, that is just
how he speak.
Last night, he kissed my mouth.

(*Not a beat taken*)

MABEL:
I am not a preacher yet.

REVEREND JOHN JACK:
Miss Peanut Brittle seem to think different.

MABEL:
I am drawn to the power of word, the ability to move
folk with them.
Has a sermon ever moved you to change?
I bore witness to that a month ago, and I thought:
I want that particular function; I want that power to
move folk.

(Pause)

REVEREND JOHN JACK:
Your words are inspiring, indeed.
I am definitely moved by them.

MABEL:
Thank you.
(Pause)
Where you comin' from?

PEANUT:
He look like he coming from South Texas:
Carrizo Springs.

MABEL:
Where is that?

PEANUT:
Northwest of Laredo.

REVEREND JOHN JACK:
You been there?

PEANUT:
No, I just like maps.
You speak Spanish?

REVEREND JOHN JACK:
Poquito.

PEANUT:
We might be able to make monies from that.

REVEREND JOHN JACK:
Speaking Spanish, you mean?

PEANUT:
A fella like you speaking Spanish?
Someone would sholly pay for that particular novelty:
believe me.

MABEL:
Peanut Brittle, hush now.

REVEREND JOHN JACK:
I do not mind a little enterprisin' in a lady.

(Pause)

PEANUT:
You could sermonize in Spanish even.
For a price, of course.
We would clean up.

MABEL:
You do not charge for the gospel.

(PEANUT *takes a seat in the tall grass.*)

MABEL:
When flights of fancy hit her, she will run off with it.
She ain't left but three feet from her boardinghouse.

PEANUT:
But I been to Ellum yonder, Sister Mabel. That got to be
more than three feet, at least.

REVEREND JOHN JACK:
What is Ellum?

MABEL:
The hood adjacent.
It is a place for hussies.
We venture in only to spread God's word, from time to
time, to the heathens.

PEANUT:
I was born there.

REVEREND JOHN JACK:
You were?

MABEL:
Peanut Brittle.

PEANUT:
It is a spiritual visit each time I go.
They say my mama was a can-can girl, and my daddy
played the piano. Mainly ragtime, but some classical
joints, too.
Now, there is a palm reader down in Ellum by name of
Dotte—

MABEL:
That is enough.
He is a man of God, and does not need to have an
earful on how those folks pass their time in Dallas.

(REVEREND JOHN JACK *takes a good look around the
property.*)

REVEREND JOHN JACK:
Is this the place to preach?
It is a bit empty, 'cepting that shack. That one over
there. And that one.

MABEL:
This is sacred land. And that is no shack. It is a shotgun
house. And it is all mine.
I run an intimate ministry.

REVEREND JOHN JACK:
It seems a bit vacant though, the neighborhood.

MABEL:
That is just your superficial understanding.

REVEREND JOHN JACK:
Go on.

MABEL:
Got some new neighbors over there, they was poking

around in my future pulpit.
(Pause)
Below all that sunburnt grass is deep spiritual ground
for renewal.
I can just feel it. Can you feel it?

REVEREND JOHN JACK:
Yes! Yes, I can.

MABEL:
Moving forward now:
I am planning my first revival to take place in this
neighborhood. Right over there.
Over where Pale Mary was adjusting her stepping out
hat.

REVEREND JOHN JACK:
What are you going to revive?

MABEL:
You ain't serious, is you? We gone revive—
Oh My

(REVEREND JOHN JACK *smiles, nervously.*
MABEL *stares at him.*
He is very pretty.)

(Damn)

PEANUT:
You staring at his mole, ain't you, Sister Mabel?

(MABEL *is quiet.)*

PEANUT:
I asked if you staring at the mole on his face. That is
rude, surely.
Just the other day you was fussing at me about staring
at Wanda Sutton's gigantic—

MABEL:
Peanut Brittle.   REVEREND JOHN JACK:
                                         Go on.

PEANUT:
Breasts.
(Pause)
I do not believe I will be so blessed in that department.
In the Wanda Sutton Department.
Okey dokey, I am finished!
(She leaves with a skip.)

REVEREND JOHN JACK:
You want kids?

MABEL:
I knew what my calling was early in life. I know my
devotion.
They ain't missing a preacher down in Carrizo
Springs?

(REVEREND JOHN JACK is at a loss for words.)

MABEL:
You have seen a lot of sad souls.
I can tell.
This city is in need of a cleanse. You come to the right
place.
You cleansed before, I suspect?

REVEREND JOHN JACK:
All the time, Sister Mabel.

MABEL:
Good, good.
We gone clean some souls in three Sunday's time.
We gone need a tent.

REVEREND JOHN JACK:
A tent?

MABEL:
Yes, a tent. We are planning a revival, Reverend.
Where is your head at?

REVEREND JOHN JACK:
Could use some sleep, quite tired. Is all.

MABEL:
I do not mind extending my home to fellow clergy.
You can gone ahead and get settled in my ministry.

REVEREND JOHN JACK:
That is right kind of you.

MABEL:
But, lemme tell you something, Reverend John Jack:
I wait up for no one.

(REVEREND JOHN JACK *nods.*
He walks into the house.)

PEANUT:
I never seen you like a man before, Sister Mabel.

MABEL:
Where in Moses did you come from?

PEANUT:
You was messing with your hair and everything.

MABEL:
You ever wear your hair in a bun, on the top of your
head, with bobby pins?

PEANUT:
No'm.

MABEL:
Well, if you did, you would scratch, too.

PEANUT:
Looked more like a primping, just kind of adjusting
some hair, a little pat here and there.

(MABEL *takes a moment, she needs one.*)

MABEL:
If you do not mind, Miss Peanut:
I got more prep to do:
(She shakes the tambourine in a quiet fury.)
His breath moved in me.
His kiss moved in me.

He touch my neck and I went hysteric.
Have you ever gone hysteric?
It is terrifying yet pleasant.
I lost my self that moment.
I lost my soul that day.
Felt within my body, movement.
Felt within my belly, result.
Felt within my heart, lament.
Song finished.

(OLIVER *stands in the middle of the road,*
not too far from THALIA, STREETER, MABEL *and* PEANUT.
Waiting for something, someone.
He burns a bunch of newspapers, just because.)

(*A different day*)

(*A giant mound of dirt.*
One side of the frame to the house is now standing.
THALIA *and* STREETER *are shoveling dirt from the mound*
around the frame.
She no longer wears her mink stole,
but wears a gardening hat.
He wears an eye patch.
They both look a bit ragged.)

THALIA:
That just seems a bit off to me.

STREETER:
Ever build a house before?

THALIA:
No.

STREETER:
This is just how long it takes.

THALIA:
But one frame only?

(THALIA *and* STREETER *continue shoveling dirt.*)

STREETER:
Your hair looks nice.

THALIA:
It is a smart bob, yes.
I look city though, right? Like I can own some shit?

STREETER:
Yes'm.
(He continues to shovel.)

(THALIA leans up against her shovel, looking out.)

THALIA:
What is all that fabric blowing in the wind?

STREETER:
Prolly just the day's laundry.

THALIA:
I say, that is a lot of clothes. What, she washing all the
clothes in the city?
(She grabs a hold of her stomach.)

STREETER:
You alright there?

THALIA:
Bellyache.

STREETER:
All that worrying over one frame.

THALIA:
No, not that.

STREETER:
Tired of sleeping in the bed of the truck?

(THALIA nods, "yes"
But:)

STREETER:
What else?

THALIA:
Worried about this loan.

STREETER:
What about it?

THALIA:
I will need to pay back the installment.

STREETER:
And, we will.

THALIA:
We? What are you gone do, place bets on ten thousand
horses, and hope?

STREETER:
Sometimes, I win.

THALIA:
Mostly, you do not.

STREETER:
Horse races ain't my thing no way. Plenty of dominoes
to wash around this city, I am sure.
(Pause)
What happen in the bank?

THALIA:
I got paper.

STREETER:
I know all that, but from where I was crouched, I could
not see nothing. Did not hear a thing.
They ask what you want to build?

THALIA:
I say a home.

STREETER:
They ask how you was gone pay back the installment?

THALIA:
Of course, they did.

STREETER:
What you say on that?

THALIA:
I say that I am to start teaching science to the high
schoolers, next fall.

STREETER:
Well, that is true.

(THALIA *sits down.*)

STREETER:
Say anything else?

THALIA:
I say my intended is an accountant.

STREETER:
I can be an accountant. I am good with numbers.

THALIA:
You are good with numbers, yes—for domino playing.
You cannot be an accountant.

STREETER:
Sure, I can.

THALIA:
In good faith:
you cannot be an accountant, Streets.
Ain't nobody gone let you do that without an
education.
Be real about yourself.

STREETER:
I can make dough, Thalia.

(THALIA *gives* STREETER *a look.*)

THALIA:
That stands to be tested.
Here, have a break.

(STREETER *puts down the shovel and goes to* THALIA.
She hands him the water jug.
She looks to her side and spots a wash basin.)

THALIA:
Where did this wash basin come from?

STREETER:
Hell, if I know.
People, things:
have a way of just appearing round here.

THALIA:
Use some of that water to get that soil off your head.
Though who can tell the difference, really.

(STREETER *pours water onto his head and shakes it off. When*
he straightens up, he is facing REVEREND JOHN JACK.)

STREETER:
The hell.

REVEREND JOHN JACK:
Excuse me, brother. I did not mean to cause no alarm.

STREETER:
Then why you creepin' up like some sort of a boxcar
villain?

THALIA:
He is apologetic, Streeter. Let it rest.

REVEREND JOHN JACK:
Well, hello, ma'am.

THALIA:
Hello.

REVEREND JOHN JACK:
How are you on this day?

THALIA:
Fine, I suppose. Shovelin' dirt.

REVEREND JOHN JACK:
Looks like you've plans for this land.

THALIA:
Yessir. Building a nice, quaint house.

REVEREND JOHN JACK:
But, how would you be able to do that? I mean, excuse
my prying, but:
a woman cannot own property, and that is something I
know without having to consult the good book.
Do you have documents?

THALIA:
I have documents.

STREETER:
Thalia, I think we need to get to the rest of our
business. Excuse us, sir—

REVEREND JOHN JACK:
Reverend John Jack. I did not quite catch your name.

THALIA:
Thalia. This here Streeter.

STREETER:
Reverend John Jack, you say?

REVEREND JOHN JACK:
I did.
Y'all just move here?

THALIA:
We did, yessir.

REVEREND JOHN JACK:
Me, too.

STREETER:
From whereabouts?

(REVEREND JOHN JACK *freezes up for a bit because:*
he does not know what to say.)

STREETER:
How you makin' out over there, Rev? You look frozen
right on through.
You ain't got to answer the question, shit.

REVEREND JOHN JACK:
I will manage. Just a little heat exhaustion, I suspect.

THALIA:
It is a hot March.

STREETER:
It is, indeed.

THALIA:
You know, Reverend:
you are actually the first clergy we done met since
coming here.

REVEREND JOHN JACK:
You have not met Sister Mabel?

STREETER:
We have not.

REVEREND JOHN JACK:
She lives down yonder in that shotgun shack.

THALIA:
She gotta a lot of laundry down there.

REVEREND JOHN JACK:
She is sewing a great, big tent.

STREETER:
Really? Why?

MABEL:
I am planning a revival.

STREETER:
Folks sure do just pop-up round here..

MABEL:
Mabel Jennings. I live down yonder.

STREETER:
Streeter. This here Thalia.

(THALIA *extends her hand to* MABEL.
MABEL *declines, giving her a side eye.*)

MABEL:
Looks like you settling in.

THALIA:
Trying our best, yes.

MABEL:
You got documents?

REVEREND JOHN JACK:
She say she do.

MABEL:
Interesting, indeed.
Ya'll together?

STREETER:
We drove up from Waller County. Ain't that right,
Thalia?

THALIA:
We sure did, Streeter.

MABEL:
Oh, my:
country folks. How fun.
Are you hitched? Married? Otherwise?

THALIA:
That is awfully personal.

MABEL:
I have never known a woman to keep a marriage so
secret.
Surely, he is not the butler, has he done it? I mean, I
would find it impossible a woman, with your look, in
her late twenties, I do suspect—with all the knowledge
God done honored me with—unmarried in the early

1920s.

(Pause)

What is really going on here?

(THALIA burps, from the pressure.
All are quiet.)

STREETER:
When did you eat chicken?

(Silence)

THALIA:
With this being tornado alley and all, I fear a twister
coming on through.
Reverend John Jack, please:
bless this soil to steer that weather on away from my
claim.

REVEREND JOHN JACK:
Let us join hands, and pray all that ill weather away.

MABEL:
Yes, let us do just that.
Let us pray to steer that awful weather away from my
revival spot.

(THALIA looks at MABEL.)

THALIA:
What do you mean by that? Your revival spot?

(Meanwhile, from down the way,
PEANUT and OLIVER are looking at the adults.)

PEANUT:
How much you wanna bet they gone brawl?

OLIVER:
Not taking that bet.

PEANUT:
Oh!

(Meanwhile, REVEREND JOHN JACK *has gathered them all in a circle. They all have their eyes closed.)*

REVEREND JOHN JACK:
Dear Lord:
please bless this house.
Amen.

THALIA:
Would you mind expressing a bit more, Rev?

MABEL:
Oh, please do, Reverend John Jack.
A taste of Carrizo Springs is what we all need right now, in this moment.

REVEREND JOHN JACK:
I can do that, sure.
Express more:
(Pause)
Lord:
please bless this land.
And the hand
that tills the land.
Take away the sand
and lend a hand.

MABEL:
You getting there, honey.   STREETER:
                                    Is he?

THALIA:
Streeter, please.   STREETER:
                                    Now I remember church,
                                    Thalia…

MABEL:
Can we all show some respect and let this man do his work?

STREETER:
Yes'm, respect.   MABEL:
                       Go on, Rev. Bless this place.

                                       REVEREND JOHN JACK:
                                       I will do just that.

THALIA:
Bee's knees.

                       MABEL:
                       What is that:
                       bee's knees?

                                       REVEREND JOHN JACK:
                                       Flapper talk, sounds
                                       like.

MABEL:
You mean, devil talk? I knew something was a bit fish.

STREETER:
She just happy to be in the big city. Is all.

                                       THALIA:
                                       Very happy.
                                       Now, Reverend, if you
                                       could gone finish your
                                       prayer.

MABEL:
Well, we do not do the devil in the big city.
                                       REVEREND JOHN JACK:
                                       I am going to finish this
                                       prayer, right now!

STREETER:
Thalia, they do not do the devil.

THALIA:
Noted.

REVEREND JOHN JACK:
I am gone sermonize the Moses out of this land.

MABEL:
We all waitin' for it, Rev.

STREETER:
Been waiting.

REVEREND JOHN JACK:
I feel it coming, y'all.
A prayer. A prayer for us all.

(THALIA, STREETER *and* MABEL *are all looking to*
REVEREND JOHN JACK *at this point.*
He starts to shake, to catch the Holy Ghost.
Meanwhile, PEANUT *is showing* OLIVER *a pail.*)

OLIVER:
Where did you get that?

PEANUT:
I stole it from the Fair Park stables.

(REVEREND JOHN JACK *is really shaking now.*)

(*Pause*)

OLIVER:
What you think they doing now?

(REVEREND JOHN JACK *can't stop, won't stop.*)

PEANUT:
Sister Mabel is congregatin' a whole other audience
now.

OLIVER:
Looks like.

(REVEREND JOHN JACK *still shakes because he has the*
"Holy Ghost".)

STREETER:
What is all that?

MABEL:
The Holy Ghost.

STREETER:
Right, right.

REVEREND JOHN JACK:
We sermonize in a fit of shakes and shrieks where I
come from.
This place is well-saved now.

MABEL:
Never seen anything like it.

THALIA:
What did you mean by that?

MABEL:
I have never seen a man shake like that before. So full
of the spirit.

THALIA:
No.
This is my claim, not a revival spot.

MABEL:
I was here first.

(THALIA *says nothing*.)

MABEL:
Come along now, Rev. Our job is done here. We will
set up camp next week.

THALIA:
How are you gone set up camp on this claim when a
great, big farmhouse will occupy it first?

STREETER:
Wait, we're building a farmhouse?

THALIA:
We are.

STREETER:
Since when?

THALIA:
Since now.

MABEL:
Ok, then. I got you.
Wanna wager a bet?

STREETER:
Now we are talking. What we betting here? Cash
money? Or toenails?
A pair of cotton drawls? Some grits, anyone wanna bet
on some grits?

THALIA:
Streeter.

MABEL:
If I sew my tent before you construct your farmhouse,
I win.

THALIA:
And if I construct my farmhouse before your tent gets
sewn?

MABEL:
I did not say all that because you will never get to that
point.

(MABEL *and* THALIA *stand there, staring each other down.*)

REVEREND JOHN JACK:
You have a blessed day, Thalia.
Streeter.

STREETER:
Jack.

(MABEL *and* REVEREND JOHN JACK *leave.*
THALIA *breathes in deeply.*)

THALIA:
I do not feel too well, Streets.
I awoke with cold sweats the other night. I feel
nauseated throughout the day.

There is a heaviness in me.
I have never felt this type of panic.

STREETER:
Back in 1918, you thought you had rot. Is it that again?

THALIA:
I did have rot.

STREETER:
Are you a plant?

(It begins to rain hard.)

THALIA:
Go let the windows up on the truck, please.
(She shivers.)

(STREETER *puts his arm around* THALIA.
She removes it.)

THALIA:
I wish I still had my fur.

STREETER:
You traded it in to get that truck.

THALIA:
I know that.
Gone get me some lemon water, please. I am parched.

STREETER:
I could use some change. I run out.

(THALIA *hands it over to* STREETER.
He walks away.)

PEANUT:
Why y'all ain't brawled?

THALIA:
Hello.

PEANUT:
I had monies on that particular situation.

THALIA:
You did?

PEANUT:
Not really, no.

(PEANUT *joins* THALIA *under the scaffolding.*
She smiles a little.)

PEANUT:
I ain't never seen anyone build a farmhouse before.

THALIA:
I, huh.

PEANUT:
That will be a treat, surely.
(Pause)
Say,
Who was your daddy's folks?

THALIA:
My daddy was German.

PEANUT:
Do you speak it?

THALIA:
Ein bisschen.

PEANUT:
That might maybe do.
(Pause)
I like your hair cut.

THALIA:
Why, thank you.

PEANUT:
You are welcome.
(Pause)
Now, woman-to-woman:
Mabel Jennings does not like it too much that you
encroached her territory.

THALIA:
It is my claim.

PEANUT:
How so?

THALIA:
Ever heard of privacy?

PEANUT:
Not really.
I live in a boardinghouse.

THALIA:
Do you not have your own room?

PEANUT:
I do; don't mean I get privacy.

THALIA:
And, why not?

PEANUT:
Strangers come to the boardinghouse day-in, day-out,
from all parts of the Southern United States.
One time from Arizona. Some from up North.

THALIA:
You the only child in there?

PEANUT:
I am.

Getting older though.

THALIA:
Will you have to leave?

PEANUT:
No'm. I can stay.

THALIA:
Well, that is good, I suppose.

(Pause)

PEANUT:
I sleep with a knife under my pillow.

THALIA:
You do?

PEANUT:
From the kitchen, yes'm. Mrs Jefferson ain't noted yet.
I have been bleeding for three month now.
I am going to start looking like a woman, someday
soon.
Ms Dotte Langfield say I can do what I gotta do if I
need to.
(Pause)
Do mens always be lookin' at you in a certain way?

THALIA:
I, oh dear.
(Pause)
What happen to your parents?

PEANUT:
My mama died during my birth; my daddy drowned
himself not too long after.
That is what they tell me.

THALIA:
I am sorry to hear that.

PEANUT:
Why should you be? You ain't the one done it.

THALIA:
It is something you say. Is all.

PEANUT:
Folks say a lot of things.

THALIA:
Indeed.

(The rain lets up.)

PEANUT:
Do not tell Sister Mabel I find you pleasant.

THALIA:
You can be certain that I will not.
(Pause)
My mama used to tell me the world smells best after a
good rain.

PEANUT:
Smells like clay.
What happened to your mama?

THALIA:
She passed on some time ago.

PEANUT:
Do you miss her?

THALIA:
I do. If I could have her here with me now, I would
know what to do about this life.
My life.

(Pause)

PEANUT:
Did they have a big wedding?

THALIA:
My folks?

PEANUT:
Your folks, yes'm.

THALIA:
My parents never married, no:
And so, I lost my home in Waller. Least that is what the
law do provide.

I weren't legit.

PEANUT:
That shit is deep.

THALIA:
Indeed.

(Pause)

PEANUT:
Say, how would you go about having your mama
here?

THALIA:
Having her here with me, at this moment?

PEANUT:
Yes'm.

THALIA:
Just a feelin' I get sometimes. But then again, it might
just be this spot.

PEANUT:
This claim?

THALIA:
I think so, yes.

PEANUT:
You think it lucky?

THALIA:
I believe so.

PEANUT:
Very interesting.

(THALIA smiles.)

PEANUT:
Say, you wanna come see the rabbit grove?

THALIA:
The rabbit grove?

PEANUT:
Down by the creek.

THALIA:
We can do that, sure.

(PEANUT *and* THALIA *head off.*
Meanwhile, over at the five- and-dime, OLIVER *is lining up*
some glass bottles on a counter.
STREETER *enters.)*

STREETER:
Newsman?

OLIVER:
Wednesdays, Thursdays, and Saturdays only.

STREETER:
Oh?

OLIVER:
I work the five-and-dime Mondays and Tuesdays.

STREETER:
Two jobs for a youngin'?

OLIVER:
Gotta make that bread, sir.

STREETER:
Looks like.

OLIVER:
Need a change of clothes?

STREETER:
Naw, just a little rain.

OLIVER:
What can I grab you, sir?

STREETER:
Some of that lemon water.

OLIVER:
Coming right on up.
(He grabs a mason jar from and fills it with lemon water.)

STREETER:
Freshly squeezed?

OLIVER:
This early morning, mister.

STREETER:
That is right nice.
How much I owe you, son?

(OLIVER *goes off to the back.*)

STREETER:
Son?
Newsboy?

(OLIVER *does not come back.*)

DOTTE:
Guess he got other business.

STREETER:
Ma'am.

DOTTE:
New to the city?

STREETER:
Few weeks old now.

DOTTE:
Right, right.
From the country, I suspect?
You dropping your "g"s from all out of plain sight.

STREETER:
Excuse the elocution.

DOTTE:
No need to blush about it. I am from Marlin myself.

STREETER:
Know any Shermans?

DOTTE:
I know them all. Family of yours?

STREETER:
Not at all. One of 'em owes me a card table from ten

year ago.
Domino game.

DOTTE:
I will let them all know. I get back from time to time.

STREETER:
What brought you to the city?

DOTTE:
Palms.

STREETER:
Palms?

DOTTE:
I read them.

STREETER:
Huh.

DOTTE:
For money.

STREETER:
I was not arguing.

DOTTE:
It is my actual vocation.

STREETER:
We all gotta have one. Newsboy got two.

(OLIVER *comes back on with freshly baked bread.*)

OLIVER:
I got three vocations. I am also this five-and-dime's
baker. Running a little bit behind, sir.
Wanna slice, y'all?

DOTTE:
I would love one, Oliver.

(OLIVER *slices the bread and hands it to* DOTTE *in
parchment.*)

OLIVER:
There you have it, Miss Dotte.

DOTTE:
Thank you.

OLIVER:
Sir?

STREETER:
Sure.

OLIVER:
I used a bit of ground clove.

DOTTE:
I love clove.

OLIVER:
I thought it would be a nice touch.

DOTTE:
Indeed.
Delicious.

STREETER:
Is that a bit of ginger as well?

OLIVER:
It is, sir.

DOTTE:
Has a nice bite to it, Oliver.

(DOTTE *signals to* OLIVER.
He takes a glass bottle from the line and dips it into some liquid.)

OLIVER:
You in need of anything else, Ms Dotte?

DOTTE:
Two more wash basins, Oliver.

OLIVER:
Got it.
(He runs off.)

DOTTE:
What brings you to Dallas?

STREETER:
Woman and me needed a new scene.
Something a bit more fast, a bit more lucrative.
We hear of more opportunity in the city. So, we come.

DOTTE:
The city is fast, surely. Lucrative, maybe.
If it is work you looking for, and your woman pretty
enough, I might could help you on out.

STREETER:
In the reading palms business?

DOTTE:
Somewhat related, yes.
Palm read?

STREETER:
Only had enough for this lemon water.

DOTTE:
On the house, Mr…

STREETER:
Streeter.

DOTTE:
Mr Streeter.

STREETER:
Nope, just Streeter.

DOTTE:
I thought for sure it was the surname.

STREETER:
Most folks do.

DOTTE:
Family name?

STREETER:
Not at all.

DOTTE:
Funny.

STREETER:
Indeed.

DOTTE:
Right hand.

(STREETER gives DOTTE his hand.)

(Meanwhile, MABEL and REVEREND JOHN JACK have had them some sex and are rejoicing-recovering. This is all post-coital—MABEL is in full rapture. No shame, at all.)

MABEL:
Dear Lord, as I lay here with this man.
I ask you accept my desire.
I ask you afford my temptation.
For the flesh ain't nothing but a vessel.
For the vessel ain't nothing but a thing to carry on through on this earth.
For this earth ain't nothing but a stop to your Heavenly gates.
Amen.
(She begins to hum.)
I bought a pair of shoes the other day;
they did not fit
I wore them shoes anyway,
felt I been rattler bit.
I wore holes in the soles
but trudged on through;
cause I know materials ain't nothing in this world
cause I got you

Yes, Lord.
I got you.

DOTTE:

>   The lines in your hands are
>   fine.

REVEREND JOHN JACK:
You usually pray and sing afterward?

MABEL:
After what?

REVEREND JOHN JACK:
After lovemaking.

MABEL:
Is that what that was?

REVEREND JOHN JACK:
Pardon me, it has been a while.

MABEL:
Felt like an earthquake.

REVEREND JOHN JACK:
No woman has ever said that to me before in my whole
entire life.

DOTTE:

>   The curvature in the
>   middle suggest water.

MABEL:
I do believe I seen Jesus Christ over your shoulder.

REVEREND JOHN JACK:
You did?

MABEL:
He did not look too happy. A little solemn to be honest.

REVEREND JOHN JACK:
He was just standing there?

MABEL:
Yes, sugar. I could ne'er misremember all that hair.

REVEREND JOHN JACK:
Sister Mabel?

MABEL:
Reverend John Jack?

REVEREND JOHN JACK:
You really need me here for the tent revival?

MABEL:
I sho'll do, sugar.

REVEREND JOHN JACK:
But, why? Seems like you got a handle on it all.

MABEL:
I do, but:
it never hurt to have more hands for the Lord. Now do
it?

REVEREND JOHN JACK:
I do like to help.

(MABEL *smiles at this.*
But, then:)

MABEL:
Now, listen:
this was a one shot deal.
You hear me?

REVEREND JOHN JACK:
You mean the lovemaking?

MABEL:
Indeed.
(Pause)
Oh no, do not do that.

REVEREND JOHN JACK:
What am I doing?

MABEL:
Sulking.

REVEREND JOHN JACK:
I apologize. I did not know I was doing it.

MABEL:
Well, you was, sugar.

REVEREND JOHN JACK:
I will try and control it from here on out.

DOTTE:
You wake for one thing
only:

MABEL:
That is what I like to hear.

DOTTE:
(Pause)   To hear her speak.

MABEL:
Put your britches on, honey.
We got some more sewing
to do.

(REVEREND JOHN JACK
puts on his pants.   DOTTE:
MABEL *hands him a piece*   Your life line, though short:
of fabric.   has many branches:
He begins to sew.)

MABEL:
You do that nicely.   DOTTE:
                             All accumulated with time.

REVEREND JOHN JACK:
Learned from my granny.

DOTTE:
Your heart line extends all
the way cross.

MABEL:
She done taught you well.

REVEREND JOHN JACK:
Thanks.   DOTTE:
(They sew together.)   You leave your heart open.

MABEL:
Gone get me some sweet tea, will you?

REVEREND JOHN JACK:
I can do that.
(He exits, comes back on.)
You wanna come show me where it is?

MABEL:
It should be in the cooler, baby.

REVEREND JOHN JACK:
It prolly is.
But, do you wanna show me exactly where you want
me to put it? In a mason jar?
In a mug? In a goblet?
Where exactly do you want it?

MABEL:
Wait, what?

(REVEREND JOHN JACK *smiles at* MABEL *and exits.)*

MABEL:
Oh damn:
I got you.
(She follows.)

(DOTTE *has finished reading* STREETER's *palm.)*

DOTTE:
It is all right there.

STREETER:
Love?

DOTTE:
Yes, sir.

STREETER:
Well, that is good.
Love is good though, right?

DOTTE:
I did not say what it would cost you.

STREETER:
Will the cost be much?

DOTTE:
Only time will tell.

STREETER:
Do you see rot?

DOTTE:
Sweetie, no, I do not.

(OLIVER *comes up from under the counter with the basins.*
DOTTE *takes out a wad of cash, and hands him some of it.*)

OLIVER:
Thanks, Miss Dotte!

(DOTTE *is gone, with the two wash basins clanking against
each other.*)

STREETER:
How much I owe you for this lemon water, son?

(OLIVER *is gone.*
STREETER *rubs his hand.*)

(*Meanwhile,* THALIA *sits alone by the creek.*)

THALIA:
There is a screened in porch when you first enter.
To the left is the living room that opens to the dining
room; I will install french doors here.
In the old place, there were no doors to be found to any
of the rooms, and no real dining room to speak of.
I will remedy all that. I will paint the place pink, even
the kitchen.
Through the dining room, there lies a hallway with a

bathroom pushing into the far-left reach.

I will look out onto the porch, viewing the progress of the neighborhood.

I will back through the room, and to the hallway, and to the second room, and then on to the third room.

This room will be midnight blue.

(She retches.)

(Meanwhile, PEANUT has made it to the five-and-dime. She holds up the dead rabbit.)

PEANUT:
Your sharpest knife please.
I need to cut these feet off.

OLIVER:
Oh my stars, why? How is it going to hop about?

PEANUT:
I need some good fortune.

(OLIVER sees that it is dead.)

OLIVER:
But do you have to cut off its feet?

PEANUT:
We will need to borrow one of Ms Dotte's books on charms to confirm.

OLIVER:
By borrow, you mean break into to Ms Dotte's home?

PEANUT:
If that is what it takes, yes.

OLIVER:
I am not helping with that.

PEANUT:
These feet might bring your daddy back.

OLIVER:
You really believe rabbit's feet will bring back my daddy?

PEANUT:
I do.
You will not have to work three jobs no more.

(OLIVER *looks at* PEANUT. *And then to the line of glass bottles.*
He sighs.)

OLIVER:
On a second thought, I will help you on out.

PEANUT:
I like to hear that.
I need a sharper knife.

(OLIVER *goes to retrieve a knife.*
He comes back.)

OLIVER:
Sharpest we got, I believe.

PEANUT:
Very good.
Got work to do on this rabbit.

OLIVER:
You gone do it in here?

PEANUT:
Where else?

(OLIVER *dry heaves.*)

(*Another day*)

(DOTTE *flips over a tarot card.*
Her shawl is wrapped loosely around her.)

DOTTE:
What you looking for is in that lower drawer.
Just take the two drops.
Last time a woman did not heed my speech, she
wound up with triplets.

(MABEL *comes from behind the screen.*)

MABEL:
I cannot have children.

DOTTE:
I do know all that.

MABEL:
How is Daddy?

DOTTE:
He is doing alright. Still working on that tractor Buzz
Latham secondhanded to him.

MABEL:
How is mama?

DOTTE:
She good, too.
(Pause)
Xavier's fine, too.
He is excited about the new addition to the
schoolhouse. It will be finished when he starts twelfth
grade next year.
How are you gone explain who you are when he turn
twenty-five?

MABEL:
Dorothy:
He will not even need his mama by then.
Besides, I might not even be around.

DOTTE:
Will you be around tomorrow night?

MABEL:
Point taken, moving on.

(DOTTE *looks at* MABEL.)

MABEL:
Listen:
Do you think this gone work? This oil?
Will it sting?

I will not feel what I have been feelin' then? A
swelling? A rush of blood, feels like.

DOTTE:
Why are you doing this?

MABEL:
My desire is impeding my ambition.
(Silence)
I cannot have another misstep.
I need it to work.
(Pause)
He is from Carrizo Springs.

DOTTE:
You think he all that good-looking?

MABEL:
Is Lucifer one of God's Fallen Angels?
His smile looks like prayer.

DOTTE:
He really gone help you become a preacher?

MABEL:
I might end up helping him, his blessings are only at
fifteen percent.
Even so, I have let him into my home now.
(Pause)
I hear Peanut keep comin' round here.
I told her you run hussies.

DOTTE:
I wish you had not done that. At all.

MABEL:
She does not need to be coming round here.

DOTTE:
She just wants to know where her parents are.

MABEL:
They are dead.

DOTTE:
She knows that much, sis.
I been tryna locate again, converse with the dead. Is all.
I just want to help her find where they buried, at least.

MABEL:
Her heart done broke before. It will stand another.
And, then another after that.

DOTTE:
Peanut came through here about a month ago, going
on and on and on about you becoming this city's first
female preacher. Had a simper on her face that was
foreign to me, said she was hell bent on becoming your
deaconess.
Had hope, had such verve.
(Pause)
She fancies you a friend cause you let her borrow a
Sunday hat.
Might as well take that hat on back today.

MABEL:
It is the truth.

DOTTE:
You wanna talk about some truth now?

(MABEL is silent.)

*(Behind a partition, PEANUT readies herself to throw a
crystal ball in MABEL's direction, or she smashes it by
clenching her fist.*
OLIVER *grabs it out of her hand and puts it in his satchel.)*

(Back)

MABEL:
What your palm say about this woman on Wilder?

DOTTE:
Leave that woman on Wilder alone.

MABEL:
She is trying to build a farmhouse on my lot.
It is where I want my tent revival. I am resolved to it.

DOTTE:
Is it hers?

MABEL:
I want to know how she came about that property. She
got peoples? Who are her peoples? Or does she think
her shade of brown better than mine, so much so that
she can just have whatever she want, however she
want it?
(Pause)
She gets to own, and I get nothing.

DOTTE:
Is that what this is? Because you pay dues to Jimmy
Kessler for your spot? Do you live in a boardinghouse?
A brothel?
You got something then, right?

MABEL:
I believe that spot to be the vital spot for the revival.

DOTTE:
You are magnificent.

(MABEL looks at DOTTE for a moment.)

MABEL:
I know that.

DOTTE:
Then stop running round here acting like some basic
ass woman.
You have your own home, your own yard, hold the
revival there.
I cannot help you with this.

MABEL:
You cannot help? Or you will not?

DOTTE:
I will not help.
Leave it be.
Go lose your sensations.

MABEL:
Oh, go back to clanking 'round town like you the wash
basin peddler in the rough!

DOTTE:
I run a tight, clean business 'round here. I keep my
girls fresh.

(MABEL *puts the vial in her robes.*
She heads to the door in a huff.)

DOTTE:
Do not slam that door.

(MABEL *slams the door.*
DOTTE *sighs.*
She lights a candle.
A rustle from within the other room.)

DOTTE:
Peanut? That you?

(PEANUT *comes from behind the screen, with* OLIVER
following.)

PEANUT:
Yes, Ms Langfield.

OLIVER:
And Oliver Oak.

(DOTTE *looks at* PEANUT *and* OLIVER.)

DOTTE:
Gotta start locking that back door, huh?

OLIVER:
Yes'm.

DOTTE:
What ya'll want?

OLIVER:
Ma'am?

DOTTE:
Well, if you busting into my quarters, you must be in need of something.

PEANUT:
What does curatorial serendipity mean?

DOTTE:
Happening by design. Why?

(OLIVER hands DOTTE the book.)

DOTTE:
You countin' thievery in your list of transgressions, too.

PEANUT:
I thought it might have something to do with good luck. Is all.
(Pause)
I do not mind that you deal in hussies.

DOTTE:
Did you hear anything else?

PEANUT:
No'm.

(OLIVER gives PEANUT a look.)

PEANUT:
We will be on our way now that we know what curatorial serendipity is.

DOTTE:
You plan on makin' some shit happen?

PEANUT:
I do, yes.

DOTTE:
Want some guidance?

PEANUT:
We will make do.
Right, Oliver?

OLIVER:
Prolly not.

(PEANUT *flicks* OLIVER *with her fingers.*)

OLIVER:
I believe in us.

PEANUT:
Bye, Ms Dotte Langfield;
you have a blessed day.

(OLIVER *and* PEANUT *leave.*
DOTTE *watches them go.*
She notices something else missing.
She lets out another sigh.)

(*A glass breaks.*
DOTTE *picks up her pistol.*)

DOTTE:
State your business in my home.

REVEREND JOHN JACK:
I hear you the lady with all the potions.

DOTTE:
I am.

REVEREND JOHN JACK:
I am in need of one.

DOTTE:
Sit.

(REVEREND JOHN JACK *does so.*)

DOTTE:
Why did you not just knock? You do know I have the
right to shoot your head off in these parts?

REVEREND JOHN JACK:
All apologies, I am new to town.

(DOTTE *nods.*)

DOTTE:
How is your stay with Sister Mabel working out?

REVEREND JOHN JACK:
Talk of the town, I reckon?

DOTTE:
No, not really. Just the talk of this particular home.

REVEREND JOHN JACK:
Really?

DOTTE:
That woman is going to be the first female to minister
in all of Dallas County. What makes you think she
wants to discuss her house guest with anyone but her
sister?
(Pause)
What you in need for, Reverend?

REVEREND JOHN JACK:
I need a repel spell.

DOTTE:
A repel spell?

REVEREND JOHN JACK:
Yes, ma'am:
a repel spell. I need a rest.

DOTTE:
From my sister?

REVEREND JOHN JACK:
I feel like a ham hock.

DOTTE:
That it?

REVEREND JOHN JACK:
I really think I can win her heart if she is not
concentrating on my body, only.

DOTTE:
Do you not want a love spell?

REVEREND JOHN JACK:
I want this all to happen, organically.

DOTTE:
Sure, okay.

*(Meanwhile, PEANUT and OLIVER have unfolded the tent for
the revival.*
She takes out her knife and begins to tear into the fabric.)

OLIVER:
Sister Mabel is not going to like that.

PEANUT:
Fuck Sister Mabel.
(She looks at him.)

OLIVER:
What's up?

PEANUT:
We are going to raise my parents from the dead.

OLIVER:
Wait, what?

PEANUT:
This revival has become a resurrection.

*(PEANUT continues to tear into the fabric, with a cigarette
dangling from her mouth.*
OLIVER butters a piece of bread and eats it.)

(Meanwhile, DOTTE is washing out some basins.
THALIA appears at the door.)

DOTTE:
I been waiting for you.

THALIA:
You have?

DOTTE:
I saw y'all roll up in your car some time ago. Did not think it would take you this long to find me, I gave him my address and everything.

THALIA:
That is a bit unnerving.

DOTTE:
You should do alright in this city, your clothes are all tattered though.
Gotta an extra corset in the back, should fit you right nice.

THALIA:
I am not here for work.

DOTTE:
Then what are you here for, honey?

THALIA:
I have not eaten in days. I have shortness of breath.
I fatigue. I burp, I dry heave, I am uneasy, emotionally.

I am pregnant.

DOTTE:
You pregnant?

THALIA:
I am.
I think it God's baby.

DOTTE:
Excuse me.

(DOTTE *laughs out loud for a really, really long time.*
THALIA *will join in, every once in a while, just as a*

somewhat involuntary thing.
DOTTE *straightens her shawl and straightens up.)*

DOTTE:
Honey, that is new to me.
That is just—
woo!
Out of sight. And I see things:
for real.
Listen:
are you a qualified virgin?

THALIA:
I am.

DOTTE:
Is this an actual thing?

THALIA:
I am not married.

DOTTE:
Do you need to be married to have sex?

THALIA:
In 1921:
you do.

DOTTE:
I got plenty of ladies round here, who ain't married,
having them some sex.

THALIA:
Are they can-can girls?

DOTTE:
They are not.
(Pause)
Honey, what do you think sex involves?

THALIA:
What do you mean?

DOTTE:
Holy moly, here we go.

(Meanwhile, STREETER sits in the bed of the truck.
PEANUT passes by with part of the tent.
She throws it in the bed of the truck, hitting him with it.)

STREETER:
Ma'am.

PEANUT:
Sir.

(PEANUT and STREETER look at each other for a while, until
it becomes somewhat of a staring contest.)

PEANUT:
I do not blink, sir.

STREETER:
Neither do I.

PEANUT:
Is that a condition?

STREETER:
No. I just have a very moist eye.

PEANUT:
I think that might maybe be a condition, sir.

STREETER:
Maybe it is.

PEANUT:
Suit yourself.

STREETER:
I turned thirty today.

PEANUT:
Is that why you look so sad and pitiful?

STREETER:
Prolly.
How old are you?

PEANUT:
Twelve; thirteen next fall.
I am a Libra.
Thirty ain't bad. I heard most mens do not even make
it.

STREETER:
Well, I did.

PEANUT:
You should be happy about that, sir. It is a blessing, for
sure.
Are you just gone sit there all day?

STREETER:
I might go down to that speakeasy.

PEANUT:
Down Ellum yonder?

STREETER:
Yep.

PEANUT:
Maybe you can have your palm read.

STREETER:
Done that today already.

PEANUT:
Ms. Dotte?

STREETER:
The same one.

PEANUT:
Good stuff?

STREETER:
She say there is love, but it will come at a cost.
Been coming at a cost, feels like.

PEANUT:
Looks like.
Got heartache.

STREETER:
Years of it.

PEANUT:
Me, too.
(She strikes a match and lights a cigarette.)
Between you and me:
Sister Mabel is a fraud.
She fornicates with men.

STREETER:
Are you sure that is what you mean?

PEANUT:
I know what fornicate means, sir. And that is what she does. She got a son, too.
She not trying to become the first of anything in this city.

STREETER:
Is it Oliver?

PEANUT:
Mabel's son? No, sir.

Oliver's mama work down by the river levee.

STREETER:
I do not know what that means.

PEANUT:
It is best you don't.

STREETER:
Is it bad? Disreputable?

PEANUT:
I say. She try to catch fish all day, but there ain't no fish in that river. Never has been, never will be.

STREETER:
So, are the fish a metaphor? Does it stand for *men*, maybe?

PEANUT:
No, sir. She literally tries to catch fish with a fishing
pole. There are no fish in that river.
Not since the Great Flood of 1908.

STREETER:
How is that?

PEANUT:
No one will ever say.
I am sorry to hear this city is treating you so bad.

STREETER:
It is not so much the city.
I thought if we came here, Thalia would be different.
Maybe need me a little more; like, if she e'er feel
sorrow, I can listen to her say things about what pained
her and why.
And, not just try and build her a house.
Three year ago, back in 1918, I held her hand in mine,
for the first time:
she somehow developed rot.

PEANUT:
What is rot?

STREETER:
It is a disease that affects plants only.

PEANUT:
Wow. That is insane, sir.
(Pause)
You wanna help with this revival? Relax your mind a
bit?

STREETER:
Not sure if I could be of any use.

PEANUT:
Don't talk about yourself that way, sir.

STREETER:
I am serious now. I cannot even use a hammer.
But, I can do long division like an adding machine. You
ever hear of a polynomial?

PEANUT:
I have actually.
How was you planning to build this farmhouse?

STREETER:
I was hoping it would take so long and fail completely,
eventually she would go on and marry me.
We would just settle somewhere else. We cannot go
back to Waller, that house is took.

PEANUT:
Between you and me, sir:
she just do not seem the type to break.
Maybe you should marry, Sister Mabel.
(What?)
Just a suggestion.
(A type of pause)
Mister, what happen to your eyeball?

STREETER:
A cat did scratch my cornea.

PEANUT:
A cat done that?

STREETER:
I tried to bandy some cats together and sell them to a
fella I know down the way.
Got cat scratched.

PEANUT:
I think you need a ritual, bring you some good fortune.
Because selling cats, sir?
There just gotta be a better way to make bread.

STREETER:
What kind of ritual?

PEANUT:
That is your call.
I have some rabbit left over from an experiment.
You can use it.
(She dashes out her cigarette.)
You can take the left-over rabbit, do a ritual, and see if
she comes around.
Or, you might come across a lotta cash.
No promises though.

STREETER:
I, okay.

(PEANUT looks over the neighborhood.)

PEANUT:
I am Peanut Brittle, by the by.

STREETER:
Streeter.

(Meanwhile, OLIVER is staring at the dead rabbit.
He thinks it moves.
He yelps.)

(Meanwhile, DOTTE has her hand on THALIA's belly.)

DOTTE:
Darling, I do not feel a thing 'cepting your heartbeat.

THALIA:
The baby's heartbeat, you mean.

DOTTE:
Naw, chile. Your heartbeat, it is racing like a
greyhound.

THALIA:
Why would my heartbeat be in my stomach?

DOTTE:
That is beyond my particular expertise.

THALIA:
And, what is your particular expertise? *Just* seeing
things?

DOTTE:
I see many things, yes.

THALIA:
You have a third eye?

DOTTE:
Only need two.

THALIA:
If I am not pregnant, then what am I?

DOTTE:
Scared sick.

THALIA:
I have never been scared in my whole entire life.

DOTTE:
Why are you building a farmhouse?

THALIA:
I need a home.

DOTTE:
Most have shotgun homes 'round Queen City.

THALIA:
I do not want to be most.

DOTTE:
And you ain't.
You moved yourself into an all black part of town, but
I am only too sure you have been mistaken, otherwise.
What, you hate yourself, but not all the way?

THALIA:
I do not hate myself. I came to this city because I hear
of better opportunity.
But, then I see how we live, and my heart just fell.
I want more than just a shack. Then just a shotgun

home.
(Pause)
And so, every once in a while, I will not correct if
someone think me otherwise.
I lost things back in Waller because of confusion, but is
it wrong to gain an advantage in this city anew, by use
of that confusion?
(Pause)
Why do you run hussies?

DOTTE:
Come again.

THALIA:
These wash basins. Does your soul not feel wretched?

DOTTE:
I do what I do to survive. Not everyone wants to know
what the future hold.
However, some are willing to spend they green on
girls.
I just take that green.
(She gets up to dry the wash basins.)
Now, if your country ass ain't got more clever things
to say about the current economic and moral climate of
both the American South and Southwest:
I got fellas coming 'round here in a few, and I gotta
dispense lavender to the ladies.
It makes the men go wild, and they spend they pockets
more.

(Silence)

THALIA:
What do you do, Ms Dotte, to let it all out?

DOTTE:
Let what all out?

(In front of the single frame of the house:
PEANUT *has a dug a hole.*

She tosses the rabbit's head into it.
She covers it up.
She waits.)

(Meanwhile, MABEL *is up and dressed.)*

REVEREND JOHN JACK:
You know if we got married, we could be a reverend couple.

MABEL:
I do not think that would work out all right.

REVEREND JOHN JACK:
And why not?

MABEL:
I have a divine purpose, in this life, on this earth.
You are really junking that all on up.

REVEREND JOHN JACK:
But we keep doing it.

MABEL:
That is not a good enough reason to get married.

REVEREND JOHN JACK:
I have fallen in love with you.

MABEL:
I think you should go.

REVEREND JOHN JACK:
I believe there a foundation, here.
So, no.

*(*MABEL *holds her hands together in prayer.*
REVEREND JOHN JACK *does the same.)*

MABEL:
Dear Lord, please tell this man to get on up, out of my chambers:
I require no more.

REVEREND JOHN JACK:
And, Dear Lord, to counter all that:
I like a woman who takes control.

(MABEL *looks at* REVEREND JOHN JACK.)

MABEL:
Oh, be quiet.

REVEREND JOHN JACK:
Love it.

MABEL:
I do not have time for this today.

REVEREND JOHN JACK:
Do you want to make time for it?

MABEL:
I do not.
The revival is tomorrow. I do not need your assistance
no more.

REVEREND JOHN JACK:
I have gotten used to this role.

MABEL:
You will need to find another one.

REVEREND JOHN JACK:
Can I bring you some sweet tea?

MABEL:
No.

REVEREND JOHN JACK:
Do you need me to press the tent?

MABEL:
I do not.

(REVEREND JOHN JACK *looks at* MABEL.)

REVEREND JOHN JACK:
But what will I do now? Where will I go?

MABEL:
I cannot tell you all that, honey.
(She gets up to leave.)
Be well.
(She leaves.)

(REVEREND JOHN JACK watches MABEL go.)

(Meanwhile, DOTTE and THALIA are howling at the moon.)

*(A day later.
THALIA and STREETER look at their progress
from the days before.
One more side of the house is up.).*

THALIA:
It looks good.

STREETER:
It really does.

(A low hum.)

THALIA:
I am proud of us, Street.
This is a new beginning.

STREETER:
You think?

THALIA:
I do.
(Pause)
What is the first thing you wanna do when we build
the rest of it?

STREETER:
Take a bath.

(A low hum)

THALIA:
Oh, good God, yes:
it has been rough without adequate running water.

STREETER:
Indeed.
(Pause)
Here that hum?

THALIA:
I do, what is that?

(PEANUT *walks around* THALIA *and* STREETER *in a circle,*
followed by OLIVER.)

PEANUT:
As I circle thee I bring forth the souls.
As I circle thee I ask for life.
As I circle thee I ask to bring dead alive.

THALIA:
What is this?

STREETER:
I think it is a ritual.

THALIA:
I can see that.

PEANUT:
We are raising my parents from the dead.

STREETER:
Wait, what?

OLIVER:
And bringing my daddy back to this city.

THALIA:
This is clearly a game.

PEANUT:
I hear this spot is vital for revival. And that is what I
intend to do.

THALIA:
Fetch me a rock, Streets.

STREETER:
You cannot go around hitting children with rocks.

THALIA:
Fine, fine.
(She looks at PEANUT.*)*
Please go home.

PEANUT:
I am resolved to this resurrection.

        STREETER:
        A resurrection?

                OLIVER:
                Indeed, sir.

        STREETER:
        I thought it a revival.

                OLIVER:
                Change of plans,
                sir.

THALIA:
Oh, dear. Did that preacher woman send you here?

PEANUT:
Sister Mabel has fallen from my favor and will not be
joining us this resurrection.
Just continue to follow behind me as I make circles
around the sacrifices, Oliver.

*(*OLIVER *takes out a sagebrush from his burlap sack.)*

STREETER:
Wait, are we the sacrifices?

            THALIA:
            I suspect we are.

OLIVER:
Am I brushing behind you with this?

PEANUT:
Brush all this dirt away.

> THALIA:
> Please do not mess with
> my dirt.

STREETER:
We done brought it all the way from the country.

OLIVER:
Now, what exactly does that mean?

STREETER:
We got into a truck, drove three hundred miles
southeast, loaded up the truck with all this soil.
And hauled it back to the city.

OLIVER:
Is that a job I can have in the foreseeable future?

STREETER:
It prolly is.

OLIVER:
I will keep that in mind.
Thank you, sir.

(PEANUT *takes a smudge stick and lights it.*
She continues to walk in a circle,
letting the smoke trail behind her.)

STREETER:
What is this?

THALIA:
Looks like a cleansing?

STREETER:
They are serious.

PEANUT:
As polio.

(*The clouds darken.*)

THALIA:
Oh, what now!

(Lightning)

THALIA:
Stop that right now! Put that book down! You are
cursing my house!

PEANUT:
This is no curse.

OLIVER:
Oh, Peanut…
Is lightning part of it?

>   PEANUT:
>   The book says it is
>   powerful.

STREETER:
I cannot say I am not a little intrigued.

(REVEREND JOHN JACK watches from outside the circle.)

OLIVER:
Maybe we should stop.

THALIA:
Please do.

PEANUT:
I will not stop.
I need my parents guidance.
I need protection.
I will no longer need knives.
I need to raise my parents today.

(A loud clap of thunder)

REVEREND JOHN JACK:
Ya'll seen Mabel?
I was hoping to get back together.

OLIVER:
I ain't overheard nothing on her wanting to get back together, kinfolk.

THALIA:
Y'all together?

REVEREND JOHN JACK:
For a short amount of time that was righteous and pure and quite unexpected.

(PEANUT *holds up the decapitated rabbit.*
She puts on a necklace of its feet.)

PEANUT:
Behold!
The sacrificial beast!

STREETER:
What is that?

OLIVER:
She killed a rabbit for this ritual.

REVEREND JOHN JACK:
With her bare hands?

OLIVER:
Yessir.

THALIA:
This is out of control.

PEANUT:
I been out of control since 1909.

(THALIA *approaches* PEANUT.)

THALIA:
Can we talk, Peanut?

PEANUT:
Make it swift.

THALIA:
This is my property, sugar. I own this. Now, your

ritual has caused enough damage, and I can forgive
that. But, there are absolutely no animals allowed on
this property.

PEANUT:
It is not alive, ma'am.
I killed it.

THALIA:
I can see that.
But, what I cannot see is how you are going to bring
your parents back by lopping off its feet.
What is gone is gone:
the past does not come back.

STREETER:
Oh, Thalia.

PEANUT:
You are building a replica of your old farmhouse.

THALIA:
Come again?

PEANUT:
You say it down at the rabbit grove.
It is a thing you hold onto, something from your past.
A relic.
(Pause)
I want my parents back.

THALIA:
But what makes you think this the place to do?

PEANUT:
You said this claim lucky when you say you wanted
your mama back to come fix your life for you.

STREETER:
You did?

THALIA:
Oh, dear. I was just expressing my discontent with my
life. Is all.

STREETER:
Discontent? With what?
With me?

THALIA:
Are we doing this now?   PEANUT:
                                I am holding a resurrection.
                                Sister Mabel has gone off
                                somewhere, and I am left
                                to get shit done.

(A tuxedo cat stands next to THALIA.
She looks down and sees it.
She begins to panic.)

*(*MABEL *enters with the tent.*
REVEREND JOHN JACK *is thrilled.)*

MABEL:
It is Sunday three, y'all.
What is all this?
(Pause)
Peanut?

PEANUT:
Mabel.

MABEL:
Sister Mabel.

PEANUT:
I know what you do.
You are wanton.

MABEL:
What did you just say to me?

OLIVER:
She say you is wanton, Sister Mabel. That is just what I

heard. I do not even know what that means.
What does that mean?

PEANUT:
She has fornicated.

(STREETER *notices* THALIA.)

MABEL:
And?

PEANUT:
What kind of preacher can you ever be now?

MABEL:
Listen:
I am a grown ass woman. I can have sex. I can do that.

PEANUT:
But, you will never have the Lord.
This is now my resurrection space.

(PEANUT *takes out a lighter.*
DOTTE *appears.*)

DOTTE:
What is all this?

OLIVER:
Peanut is raising her parents from the dead.

(*Spotting the sagebrush*)

DOTTE:
Well, now I know where the missing sagebrush gone
off to.
(*Pause*)
Sweetie, I do not think you know what you are doing
here.

PEANUT:
I beg to differ.
(*She drops the smudge stick on top of the buried rabbit,
wherever that is.
She lights the sagebrush and sets it behind her.*)

(THALIA *visibly shakes.*
DOTTE *looks on.*)

STREETER:
Thalia?

> PEANUT:
> And she wept.
> And she knew in her heart
> how much they had missed
> her to raise her.
> And they all came to greet
> her.
> But, she did not feel the
> same.
> She had transformed,
> somehow

STREETER:
She is shaking all over.

DOTTE:
Oh lord:
(*She goes over to* PEANUT.)
Peanut, you cannot use a sagebrush to raise the dead.
That is not what you use it for. It causes nervous
disorders.
Dry heaving, in high dosages.

(THALIA *dry heaves.*)

STREETER:
Are you okay?

> THALIA:
> Where is that cat?

> OLIVER:
> It went across the
> road to join the
> other cats.

THALIA:
Wait a minute. Other cats?

STREETER:
Those cats ain't worried about you.

THALIA:
You keep saying that, but it is not true.

OLIVER:
There are about thirty of them, at least.

> DOTTE:
> Peanut, I want you to stop
> all this.
>
> PEANUT:
> She was not as they
> remembered her in life.

(MABEL *sees* REVEREND JOHN JACK.)

MABEL:
Were you hiding?

REVEREND JOHN JACK:
I have been standing here this entire time.

(*Everyone looks to* REVEREND JOHN JACK.)

MABEL:
Gonna proclaim love again?

REVEREND JOHN JACK:
I forgot my hat.

MABEL:
Does it look like it grew legs, and is running away
from you?

REVEREND JOHN JACK:
It does not.
(*He grabs his hat.*
He looks at them all.)
Which way to Union Station?

OLIVER:
Three and a half mile west of here.

(REVEREND JOHN JACK *makes to leave but sees* MABEL.
As she unfolds the tent, seeing that it is torn:)

MABEL:
What is all this?

OLIVER:
I am so sorry, Sister Mabel.

MABEL:
Did you do this?

OLIVER:
...no.

(MABEL *looks over at* PEANUT.)

PEANUT:
She was full of fury.

MABEL:
(To PEANUT*)* Why did you do this?

(THALIA *looking at* MABEL.)

THALIA:
You kept a watchful eye on us this entire time,
questioning our relationship.

MABEL:
I kept a watchful eye on the spot I desired for my
religious transformation.

(The fire has begun to slowly grow.
Thalia grabs an end of the tent; Mabel holds fast.
A tug of war begins between Thalia and Mabel.)

THALIA:
I have never even had sexual intercourse.

(MABEL *lets go of the tent, sending* THALIA *flying.)*

OLIVER:
Whoa!

STREETER:
Hold your wisdom, girl.

MABEL:
How did that even happen?

REVEREND JOHN JACK:
Oh, brother, I am sorry to hear that.

> STREETER:
> Everything is fine.
> Alright.
> It is gone be alright.

REVEREND JOHN JACK:
But, you building this woman a house?

> STREETER:
> I am in love with this woman.

OLIVER:
It works that way?

STREETER:
It can.

OLIVER: PEANUT:
Oh, wow.   And they could not forget what they
                                 had seen.
                                 They had watched her rise.
                                 And rise.

DOTTE:
Anyone else got something to say?

REVEREND JOHN JACK:
I have a confession to make.
I am a day laborer from Mesquite. Haven't stepped
foot in a church since age three.
We were passin' through Dallas on our way to Waco,
and I just thought it so nice.
So I just did not get back on the truck.

Is all.
Never gave a sermon in my whole entire life.

STREETER:
That makes sense.

THALIA:
Oh, what next?

(The frame collapses around all seven, hurting none.)

THALIA:
Of course.
Of course.
Of course.   OLIVER:
Of course.   This house done broke
Of course.   her.
I cannot believe all this shit.

(DOTTE sees the fire for the first time.)

DOTTE:
This place is catching on fire.

(MABEL sees the burning tent.)

MABEL:
My revival is in flame.
(She is bereft.)

STREETER:
We need to get out of here.

THALIA:
What happens to my claim?
This was all I had in the whole entire world.

(STREETER looks at THALIA, while leading her off.)

DOTTE:
Oliver?

OLIVER:
Yes, Ms Dotte?

DOTTE:
Go see if the fire fighters will come to our part of town.

(OLIVER *is off.*)

DOTTE:
Mabel, you have got to get yourself out of here.

(MABEL *leaves.*)

REVEREND JOHN JACK:
Downtown?

DOTTE:
Over northwest.

PEANUT:
She was full of a sorrow
that was neverending.

REVEREND JOHN JACK:
Thanks, ma'am.

She was full of a rage that
would not quell.
Taken was she so early.

(REVEREND JOHN JACK *is off.*)

PEANUT:
With everything in my heart:
raise the dead.
With everything in my soul:
raise the dead.

DOTTE:
Peanut:
it will not work, honey. It will not work.
Once a person dies, that is it. They do not come back.
The body decomposes, and it stays with the earth.

(PEANUT *runs off.*
DOTTE *lets out long sigh, that is filled with a hundred
pounds of regret as she has broken a child's heart.
She leaves as the fire grows.
Night falls.
Time passes.*
DOTTE *and* MABEL *sit at a table with tarot cards.*
DOTTE *flips a card.*)

DOTTE:
No.

MABEL:
Flip another one.

DOTTE:
The cards say, "no", Sis.

MABEL:
Was it ever part of a design? Becoming a preacher?

DOTTE:
No, honey.

MABEL:
Then I guess that is that.

DOTTE:
Is that really what you wanted?

MABEL:
I want authority over my own life.
(*Pause*)
I gave birth to a baby boy out of wedlock, and I gave
him away.
I take pleasure in sex. I have never felt the need to
marry.

DOTTE:
You knew your limits in taking care of Xavier. So, you
gave him away to mama and daddy.
You may not ever become Dallas's first female
preacher, but you are ahead of your time, in some
respects.

(MABEL *smiles a little.*
DOTTE *flips a card.*)

DOTTE:
Lovers.

MABEL:
Keep going.

(Pause)

DOTTE:
How you feelin'?

MABEL:
The same.
I feel amorous. I feel sexual things. I am a sexual being.
It all feels normal.

(DOTTE *nods.*)

DOTTE:
You wanna work here?

MABEL:
Hell no.
I would rather keep laundering clothes.
When a man pay for it, he act like he got a say in the
matter.
Shit.
I know what I like.

DOTTE:
Just a bit of tommyrot.

MABEL:
Unh uhn.

(Pause)

DOTTE:
There is a new railroad coming through.

MABEL:
Oh?

DOTTE:
Yes'm.

MABEL:
Muscles.

DOTTE:
Indeed.

(PEANUT *appears at the door.*)

PEANUT:
Is it okay for me to come in?

DOTTE:
Come on in.

*(*PEANUT *looks at* MABEL.*)*

PEANUT:
Mabel.

MABEL:
Peanut.

PEANUT:
I am apologetic that I burned down your sacred plot
with that sagebrush.
(She looks at DOTTE.*)*
And I am apologetic that I took your sagebrush and
burned it.
Please allow me to replace it with this weeping willow
branch.
(She places the branch on the table.)
The willow can bend itself in various contortions,
without snapping.
You can eat its bark, it is nutrient.

DOTTE:
I am sorry your resurrection did not go very well.

(PEANUT *shrugs.*)

MABEL:
Me, too.

PEANUT:
But I hijacked your revival.

MABEL:
You did, yes.
I suppose it weren't much of revival, no ways.

(PEANUT *hands her a bit of tent.*)

PEANUT:
Here's this.

(MABEL *looks at it.*)

MABEL:
What is this, a keepsake?

PEANUT:
It is.

MABEL:
Thank you.

(PEANUT *smiles a little.*)

DOTTE:
What time you due back at that boardinghouse?

PEANUT:
Around five.

MABEL:
Take a seat til then.

(PEANUT *takes a seat at the table.*)

DOTTE:
You got time for a palm read?

PEANUT:
I do.

(DOTTE *takes her hand.*)

DOTTE:
Where is Oliver Oak? Out selling papers?

PEANUT:
No'm. His daddy come back.

(MABEL *and* DOTTE *look at each other, a little surprised.*)

PEANUT:
Now, what is my palm telling you, Ms Dotte?
What does my future hold?
(*There are no words for what this young girl will endure.*)

(A little while after, THALIA *and* STREETER *sit on the back of the pickup truck, the torched ground below.*
Streeter's eye has healed.
Miraculously, a beam still stands.)

THALIA:
How long you think it will take for this grass to grow back?

STREETER:
Six months, maybe.

THALIA:
Six months?

STREETER:
Maybe.

*(*THALIA *sighs.)*

STREETER:
I must admit something to you:
I cannot build a house.

THALIA:
What do you mean?

STREETER:
I have never built a thing in my life.

THALIA:
Why did you lie to me?

STREETER:
I just wanted to be close to you, working side by side, going toe to toe. Is all.

THALIA:
How did that work out for you?

STREETER:
Not well.
(Pause)
Do you think you can learn to love me over time?

THALIA:
I want my children to have a chance in this life.

STREETER:
And what exactly does that mean?

THALIA:
I want them to have things.

STREETER:
Why wouldn't they have things with me as a daddy?

THALIA:
Take one look at you and take one look at me.

(STREETER *looks at* THALIA *for a while.*)

THALIA:
I do love you and value you as a friend, Streeter.

(Pause)

STREETER:
Right, right.

(STREETER *is still as* THALIA *continues on; in his thoughts.*)

THALIA:
I finally went over to Ellum the other night.
My goodness—that place hops! I have never seen so
much bustle! Or, hustle.
There was so much activity, I thought for sure the law
would shut it all down.

STREETER:
Your children will not have all the things, Thalia—with
or without me. Did you have it all?
You marched into that bank, and passed, and got
a loan for this claim; but did you leave that bank
feeling fulfilled, feeling proud? Or, was there a part of
you that felt your dignity damaged? Your humanity
undermined?
They might have some of the things, but not all the
things.

With some of those things that they do have, it will not
feel like a victory.
It will come at a cost.

THALIA:
Then I will settle for some of it.

STREETER:
Am I below settling?

THALIA:
I want my children to feel alright in the world. Do you
feel alright in the world?

STREETER:
There was this crimson shed back in Waller on our
little plot of land that had honeysuckle overgrown
in the back. I used to sit in its shade. I would take a
flower from the tree, and gently pull the stem from
the bottom, and watch the nectar ease its way down it,
with a tilt of my hand.
I would let the liquid stretch to the stem's end, but
right before the nectar reached it—and it was about to
drop off to the soil:
I would put it to my mouth.
Taste that sweet.
It was as if this was a secret ritual only I knew; like I
had a hand in all of creation.
(He finally looks at her.)
I have felt alright in this world.

(THALIA looks at STREETER.)

THALIA:
Let us tear this shit down.

STREETER:
Wait, what?

THALIA:
We certainly cannot occupy this house knowing that

my dignity was infirm while passing.
We will just tear it all down.

STREETER:
That is not where I thought you would go with that.

(THALIA *only needs to push the beam over for it fall.*
STREETER *watches it as it falls to the earth.*)

THALIA:
There is nothing I need to learn over time.
I have always loved you, Streeter.
(She opens up a picnic basket.)
Happy birthday.

STREETER:
Thank you.

(THALIA *looks around at their claim.*
She raises a fork.)

THALIA:
To Wilder.

STREETER:
To Wilder.
(Pause)
You need your parasol?

THALIA:
I do not.

(And, in this very moment, they are the only two people in the whole entire world.)

END OF PLAY

www.ingramcontent.com/pod-product-compliance
Lightning Source LLC
Chambersburg PA
CBHW052131090426
42741CB00009B/2038